LOVE'S PROMISE

COLLECTED POEMS BY:

THE GODDESS ANAHATA

LUNAR LEVELS
PUBLISHING

© 2025 LUNAR LEVELS PUBLISHING LLC

All rights reserved.
No part of this book may be used or reproduced
in any manner whatsoever,
including AI regeneration and Internet usage,
in whole or part, without written permission from the publisher,
LUNAR LEVELS PUBLISHING, except in brief quotations
embodied in central articles, editorials, and reviews.

LUNAR LEVELS PUBLISHING LLC
Louisville, KY USA

www.lunarlevelspub.com
www.thegoddessanahata.com
outreach@lunarlevelspub.com
socials: @thegoddessanahata
@lunarlevelspublishing

Design: Jeremiah J. Shelton
Authour Photograph: Mahogany M. Shelton
Cover Art: Mahogany M. Shelton

ISBN-13: 979-8-218-59057-4

Lunar Levels is a registered trademark of LUNAR LEVELS LTD. CO.

Printed in the United States of America

For my promise to Love.
For my promise to The Universe.
For everyone who keeps their promises.

THE GODDESS ANAHATA

TABLE OF CONTENTS:

CH. 1   When It Comes To You … … … … *1*
Impressions | Sunrise | A Little Taste | Bandit | Opening Act |
I See Your Mind | Grasp | Hopium | Haiku Hour Pt. 1 |
Almost | One Sound | Too Real | Chiropractor | Tiny Thoughts |
Sentient | Windchime | Together | Knee Deep |
Overheated Plastic | Mind Games | Proceed With Caution |
Organic | By DesigN | if you're sure | Un-Complex |
Are You Up For The Challenge? | Lack | Pleasure |
Just Desserts | It's Love Related | Garden | Be You | Delivery |
Skinside | Verde Día | Build | A Butterfly Beacon |
Double Direction | Traveller | What Happens In 4 | 2099 |
West | Set | Firefighter | The Last Discovery |
A Wizard Making It Disappear | Shakes |

CH. 2   Approaching Me … … … … … … *67*
Poet | Course of Action | PTO | Body of Art | Almighty |
And I Do Grow | Taking Over | Deus Ex Machina |
Speed Dial | Giver's Dilemma | Red Alert | Led By God |
Can I Still Wish? | Happy Tears | Mother | On A Mission |
All Night | Approaching | I Thank The Universe | Translation |
Wat(her) | Great In Good Taste | Challenging |
Keeper No Keeping | Gotta Count For Something | Formerly |
Answers | Encrypted | Ayudarme | Party Time | Airhead |
Natural And Easy | Mind | Million Dollar Inquiry | Enola |
How High | Way to Express | Stupid Questions |
On a Haiku Pt. 1 | 222 | Shower Therapy | Haiku Hour Pt. 2 |
Zeros and Ones | Rain On Me | Sensitive |
Now They All Love Water | Home | War |

CH. 3   Scale Out … … … … … … … *131*
Love's Leftovers | Emitting Time | Privileged | Disconnect |
Who Are You? | Misdirection | Unknown Surprises |
The Final Hour | Home Base | Too Tight | Inspired Alchemy |
Haunted House | J.F.H. | Midsummer | Dragonflies Talk |
Tomorrow | Altitude | You Only Live Forever |
Optimize & Upgrade | Post-Nuptial Disagreements |
Still Too Loud | State of Emergency | Smoke |
Because I Can See… | On a Haiku Pt. 2 | About Nature |
Toxic Positivity | Overstand/Understand |
Psychiatric Assistance | A Trillion Choices |

LOVE'S PROMISE

CHAPTER 1:
WHEN IT COMES TO YOU

Impressions

I felt you. Really FELT you.
How lonely it gets for you-
to be in love with life and still wondering what it's like
to feel what you've never had before.
The weight you carry.

It was seeing your mind mapped out,
sharing your evolution
as I traced my questions along treasure's road.
Seeing who you are be so far from who you were...
time traveling through a myriad
of experiential juxtapositions.
I almost wished I could've been there
to love you through that pain.

It was the gravitational pull of my body to yours-
hearing your heart tell me
the depths of all you'll do to keep me there.
Put my comfort on the table
and you held it tighter by the second.

What took you so long to find me?

It was how you chose not to let me go;
hand fit perfectly into the arch of my back-
a missing piece to your puzzle and mine.
It was feeling your fingertips in my hair
using "light" as a verb and a noun
for the action and sensation I hadn't felt before.

As I harmonized sweet everythings in your left ear,
it was in the vibration of your voice
telling me "yes" to all you knew you could prove.
I became your etheric anomaly in the flesh.

It was our shared gaze;
onyx looking at obsidian-
protectors in our own right,
unorthodox by design,
strong since we're built for it,
great because we have to be,
all we carry for our purpose-
patient enough for "the one" to share it with.

It was imagining what our empire would look like
as mind and heart together- one body.

It is what I feel each time replaying those moments;
our chapter start to finish.
A new book creation is in order.
So if you're ready, as the universe will see,
I'll begin my count.
And by rule of three, you'll belong to me.

Sunrise

It excites me to know
that we see the same skies,
the same strawberry sunrise
and the same sunsets.
It excites me to know
how close we can be
no matter the distance.
And it excites me to know
how we share this feeling
on the same sunrise.

A Little Taste

I need to taste your lips.
Kiss me once.
Then again.
Come again.
Run it back.
Back to back.
Lay me on my back.
Feel the heat coming from my spine
when you move your hands like that.
I'm ready for you now.
All I want is you.
What do you want me to do?
Anything, you choose.
I won't bite
unless your lips ask me to.
Kiss me as if
you only get one
to prove you love me.
What do you say?
As if this is the only way
you get to articulate.
Let your kisses marinate.
Mashallah.
Keep going,
no matter how much time it takes.

Bandit

Hands where I can see them
It's a stick up
I'm the moonlight bandit
A thief in the night
And I'll give you to the count of three
To put your past in this bag
We're burning the remnants
Because you've already got the lessons
I rob you of pain
And replace it with bandages
Reverse damage
I take stress
And alchemize the pressure
Till all that's left
Is the love you manifest
I steal from the ego
And give to the heart
I'm deebo to your doubt
Give me the identity
Of your preconceived notions
On how love exists
As I show you what healed affection is
Don't you dare move
I take everything that doesn't serve you
Call ya mammy if you want it back
Say another mf word and your hurt is over
I dig deep into your soul
Pull out all your limitations
And do the dash on you so fast
It feels like a dream
By the time you wake
You're flushed of toxins
With hands full of exotic fruit
And spiritual tonics
The moonlight bandit plays no games
Now keep those hands up high
And wrap your arms around mine
Love looks immaculate on you
To see that smile
I'll rob you as many times as I have to

Opening Act

Ooh la la, yes papá,
there's no way
for me to fathom the thought
of any other coming to cover
and take me under
because I'm only for you.
I'm what you're needing,
your soul I'm feeding,
deep chakra healing,
I'll be next to you soon
Ooh la la, Ooh la la, Ooh la la, yes papá

Midnight turned day too quick, all seconds split.
I survived til 6 am the urge
to explore hidden genealogy of your lips
and how they feel touching my hips.
With each "almost" kiss, I felt a sixth sense-
the sweetest thing I've ever known
upon my goddess throne.

My water with your fire created a deep jacuzzi,
a boiling sea of deluxe energy.
Just you close to me.
Two souls connecting cosmically.
Delightful, delectable, decadent.
The taste of your flesh such a rich flavour.
Chocolate truffles with a caramel hint.

To show the magnitude in which I've missed you,
I wanna lick pineapple juice off your tattoos
after a sip or two.
That's what blue lotus and manuka honey tea do.

With your permission,
I'll send an interstellar transmission
of psychoactive hallucinations
posed from triple dark prisms
into your temporal lobe;
a lucid aphrodisiac to make your muscles relax.

Control your stress,
trigger points I press
to relieve your nervous system
of over thinking about what's next.

Ooh la la, yes papá,
there's no way
for me to fathom the thought
of any other coming to cover
and take me under
because I'm only for you.
I'm what you're needing,
your soul I'm feeding, deep chakra healing,
I'll be next to you soon
Ooh la la, Ooh la la, Ooh la la, yes papá

Rápido,
dime telepáticamente
cuánto quieres amarme,
y cántame mientras caes en un sueño
profundo para que pueda soñar contigo.

Water may not be wet, but my primordial H_2O
is ready to make your hands and chest...
let me calm down for a sec.
Open my flood gates
and let your intentional masculinity do the rest.
Feel new highs; introducing new depths.

I See Your Mind

You can't hide it anymore.
I see your mind-
the place I have to explore.
It called to me-
louder than the lion's roar.
I see your mind-
and it's amazing.
Your thoughts speak to me
through your heart
and now I see
how much you want
to always love me.
And I see your mind.

Grasp

You're my pineapple thug passion.
Talk so nice and back it up with action.
Know exactly what you want and for it all,
I wanna tell you I love you.
You got me forever.

In my ocean are your gems, my black pearls.
We are the same infinite void
as I bathe in your gaze.
Sea of the ether.

Giving love to a god under the stars
from Neptune back to Mars,
takes charge through the dark
encapsulated in bioluminescence
by a goddess heart.

Every cloud,
moonlit night,
dancing tree shaking its leaves,
wind flowing through...
sends my love, my kisses,
my prayers and best wishes.
Know that I am near.

Remember:
there's no where
you could ever be
that I wouldn't
reach you.

Hopium

I almost prefer to just hear you talk because then
my imagination is the little engine that could
believe you're true to everything you say you'll do.

Estoy triste porque sé que no dices lo que dices en serio.
Pero quiero que tus palabras ser verdad.

I let you strum the strings of my Spanish guitar-
my fragile Colombian orchid heart,
playing sad notes of dead stars.

Put the 'h' on ate and opium,
a full stomach high off hate and hopium-
hoping you'll get it right
and growing to hate the monster you've become.
Eighth time's a charm.

But you only put on your best try,
your best suit and tie, under low party lights
when I'm sitting on your lap
with a worried face glittering from my cheek's highlight.

I like you because
of all preeminent aspirations to be honest
and love you despite an unnerving disposition
to sabotage true love with self doubt.
Pockets full but your heart is empty.

As I saunter away remembering the good times,
how the click of my heels would light up your face
and when your laugh could brighten my rainy days,
I can't stay.
I pray you value the next one from lessons of losing me.
Once my presence is missed, it'll be too late.

Haiku Hour Pt. 1

If I could translate
My words into shapes, colours, and sounds,
You'd be a living utopia dimension.

In search of synchronicities,
We comparably find
Perfect confirmation biases.

Almost

I'm so into you.
And I have another place
I want you to get into too.
But I would prefer you not view me like "that".
The kind of woman who goes easy-
who requires no chivalry, courting, or teasing.
That's not me; it's just something about you.
Wanna share my juice box and fruit snacks
under the slide after class...
if you can pick up what I'm putting down.
For I know I can't control
what your definition of respect is,
but I can ensure to embody
what's clearly worth respecting
... so I hold back.
Holding back the intrigue I have
to learn what you feel like inside me.

And I say "yield"
when all I want to say is: "go, more, and yes".
Because even though I want you physically,
I require more to the foundation of how we associate.
I have to have all of you and I won't settle for less.
I'm enthralled.
If I may, inscribe my name on your rib cage.
The gods protect all who matter to me
& melt their burdens into swords for protection.
My love is alchemy.

While I don't know your soul yet, I want to.
To know how you've become you and everything built
which makes your spirit so beautiful.

Only proof could do these words justice
but since it's just us right here,
hear me clear.
I want to know what love looks like on you
and how deeply you feel
when it comes from me.
What song do you feel as I touch you?
I want to help you transcend.

All truth, you and I, we're quite the same.
Aesthetically privileged. Visually superb.
You and I are intricately fine as can be.
Who and whatever we want is ours.
Never needing deception to lead the charge;
we just got it like that. No playing games.
Too superior to swindle hearts.

This is the honest me who honestly
desires every part of you exclusively.
I only ever wanted you since the moment we met.
Now respond with what is on your mind.
If your intentions are completely
left field from mine, that's fine;
can't hold on much longer.
Both sets of lips crave release from the suspense.
I'm falling and I need both of your arms
to be wrapped around mine.
Let me know your perspective on our time.

All that matters is how I value me,
so respect me enough to use soul stirring transparent honesty
as the decision if we explore bodies today
and weave spirits moving forward.

One Sound

My heart is like a marching band.
I've become an Outkast.
Unfamiliar to man.
But long overdue.
One sound I'm connected to.
Greatest song ever written.
I'm in the stands singing a song.
That sounds like you.

Too Real

I felt you kiss me in my dream.
More than a dream from what it seems.
Right before my eyes opened to full wake,
I felt you clear as day.
Lying on my stomach, I felt your breath...
warmly, softly...
dance between my shoulder blades.
My body between your hands,
sinking further into the memory foam
as you increased pressure.
Only separated by thin linen,
your clothes and my clothes.
Lips closer to my neck.
At the moment I became a magnet-
needing to connect my North Star
to your south node.
True love's kiss.
I wanted to turn over and see you
when my eyes opened.
The deep desire for it to be real.
To have you with me.
And I knew it wasn't a dream,
but I just couldn't see you.

Chiropractor

I'm a bit tensed up and I need to be stretched out.
Can you help me?
Turn me into taffy that gets softer as you work it.
Those hands I love so much.
Give it everything you got.

All my laces are tied and my corset is kind of tight.
Will you loosen me up?
Pull at each string.
I'll hold it in until you say breathe.
Make me release everything
I've ever wanted you to know.

I need a chiropractor.
Can you curve me proper?
Twist my spine.
My back has been aching
without your thrusts and compressions.
Teach me a lesson.
Bend my body;
engrave your name into my skeleton.

I'm trained and finely tuned
to your electric guitar.
You play the notes?
Now amplify it.
Lift my legs until they tremble.
You're the bass and I'm treble-
If I tap out, I'm in trouble.
I surrender to your love.

I remember the shiver felt when we first touched.
Do you recall?

Let me savour this. I favour it.
I saved my water lily just for you.
She calls and quivers
in urgent need of relief only you can deliver.
Kiss me out and inside.
I'm too wet.
Ring me dry so I can replenish.
Drink me slow.
Hold my waist and don't waste any.
I'll make more so take plenty.

I think I need a doctor.
Are you seeing patients tonight?
I need patience tonight.
A sequel and two nights.
Pay attention henceforth- put my soul on your roster.
Pulsing and throbbing,
a soliloquy of whimpers and hollers
is what I crave right now.
"Breathe in, bite down" -
I love when you command me.
Try my soft sighs on for size.
Peyote on your tip
and ayahuasca on my shea butter thighs.
I'm so high.

I belong to you.
Am I in a place where I can let go?
Realign and define.
Immortalize me.
Scope the scene.
Mind, heart, body: all going insane
just before the first time I came.
Now we're the same.

Tiny Thoughts

Touch me everywhere
hands wouldn't dare
and I swear
I'll make it worth your while.
Nothing can compare
to the time we share
in my mind and exploring yours.
Handle me with care
when I'm oh so bare
and I'll become yours forever.

Sentient

And I'm a siren.
But not the lustful temptation
of dangerous manipulation
drilling 808's through your ear.
I'm a special siren
who orates linguistic lullabies-
a lasting luminous love.

I picked up the cadence of your radiance;
seen it as soon as our paths crossed paths.
the volcano in you-
just stirring up and waiting
to create the most spectacular catastrophe...
a bountiful island formation
- sight beholding.
No farther can you wander without me.

I've mastered the ancient art
of Sentient Seduction.
Revealing wonderland-
a place in me for you to incubate imaginations
& ponder peacefully.

An omnipotent opulence
of quantum consciousness,
I've charmed you
into setting your soul free of love's boundaries.
How tranquil love should always feel.
And you've earned it- beyond worthy.
Your Nefertiti has conquered and seized
while, she too, submits to your godly being.
Patient love that basks in your protection.

Under my spell,
I have you suspended mid air-
poking and prodding at parts needing healing
using my love as a defibrillator,
jolting dispersed energy
into concentrated electricity...

Do you trust me to open you up? *right there*
The Most High sent me to unlock you.

Embracing this transcendence Allah made,
I found Egyptian hieroglyphs etched in my note:
"I'm in love with you"...... is what I wrote.
I mean it now just as my spirit did eons ago.

I'll trace it in the stars starting with star Sirius.
A love blessed by the ancestors hearing this-
I love that I'm in love with you.

Wind Chime

Some say you're "two faced"
but really it's just two faces breath.
The in and out breaths.
Two steps.
You breathe in to live and breathe out to avoid death.

Two sides of the same coin.
Don't they both spend the same?
... air in the night and in the day;
you still breathe the same way.

The air we need.
We KNOW it's there even though we can't see;
existing for the earth, plants, trees
bugs, animals, soil, and seeds...

One can take advantage, in your imbalance,
of what they don't appreciate enough.
Being you is tough.
Constantly living for us but when you tornado,
you wonder who's there to get your storms unstuck.

Undervalued when calm
and berated when you act unjust.
You had to learn to control the storms
and not uproot houses so much.
Balance is good but sure enough,

I LOVE YOU and I dance when wild winds get rough.

You there, a spontaneous imaginative child,
the one who moves free.
I need you all the time. The breath inside of me.

Together

He came right from the
"wish a nigga" would/woods.
A nigga that wished he would turn into a god
to find his goddess and he found her.
Hands still certified along with his super mind;
he's diligent, militant, vigilant.
To love his woman is to love god.
From her tippy toes up to the 9ether tresses,
he loves her far beyond sex
because they're playing chess.
His queen moves around in directions
he can't access
so he can focus on what's next
and she'll knock down the rest.
Together they work best.

Loving him lifts her spirit up.
When she sees the glittering reflection
of his eyes staring at her in the darkness,
everything she ever knew
about magic gets reimagined.
He is sparkling crystal,
razor sharp steel.

Loving him helps keep her emotions in line.
Not letting the downs keep her too long
so she can be herself at all times.
True to her nurturing nature.
He adds balance.

Loving her allows him to understand romance.
Encyclopedia of "how to make her smile"
is the current read.

She is fine china, a masterpiece.
With her, he is sweet
& a soldier in the street.
She creates an abundance of peace.

Loving her revives his faith in its power.
As all feels lost, she is the answer to his prayer:
if she is real, bring her forth.
His promise not to fumble.
A nomad who found home in her heart.

Knee Deep

Get deep.
So deep
that my screams turn to whimpers
of sweet relief.
More of you into
more of me.
Would you mind
getting deep?
Knee deep.
Making my breaths shallow
and scratches weak.
Can I take care of you
in every way you please?
Let me make love to a god.
Satisfying you satisfies me.
Pull me in.
Into you.
Hold me by my knees
and go
deep.

Overheated Plastic

Right now, your love is like that one half finished
stepped on bottle of water with the ripped label
that rolled from under your car seat,
left directly in the sun on a spicy July afternoon.
The bottle you frown at because it's the only thing in the car,
the store is too far, and you just did an eight mile jog...
you drink it mad as hell- insides now burning twice as hot.
You see I'm parched, but crushed plastic
is the best you claim to offer, so I sip it
like I'm not already familiar with the boiling taste.
An uncomfortable flavour of hot chemicals
I trick myself into believing might actually
still resemble good water-
only to leave me more dehydrated than I was before.
Might as well be acid slithering down my throat.
Yes, still, I pick up the bottle-
one hand beginning to melt, feeling the warning signals;
my palm's pain receptors triggered
from the hot plastic of your heart.
I untwist the cap, preparing to scold my insides,
convincing my mind this sip won't be "as" hot;
only 85° instead of 90° so "it could be worse"...
this love probably isn't refreshing but "it's something".
Even that bottle too, was once a cool drink of water.
Once upon a time, every sip quenched the thirst
of a glorious love that just needed to be chilled.
Instead of properly preserving it on ice,
I guess the better idea was to make the next one
who needed a drink suffer since the last parched lover
didn't sip and store it right.
Out the window you go
so no one else has to suffer from the taste.
Just like the trash stuck in the grass
on the highway, what a waste.

Mind Games

You'd like to peek inside my mind –
they all would;
you want to see inside my brain –
just like they all do.
So what makes you our lucky special explorer?
The angels have been up in the clouds pillow talking
again; they told you how much fun it is in here
and how just one visit
could change the rest of your years.

But if I share an inch,
prove you wouldn't try to take a mile.
P.S., the rumors are true;
these brain waves can take you on the ride of your life.
Can't let you get hooked on this good stuff –
this good love –
these fiery neurons and stellar cognitive connections.
A beautiful brain is no such playground.
Don't play around.
There will be no sneak peaks ever.
Now turn those wants into work.
Show me how you'll earn
the chance to experience this endeavour.

Proceed With Caution

I'm not scared to let you in.
I'm cautious.

I'd love to take you on a tour of my love temple.
But will you be gentle?
My heart is a jade palace
of irreplaceable art and exquisite architecture.
Maybe I'm more excited to show you
than you are to see.
I wonder if it's worth giving you a key.
I've already changed enough locks
when someone enters then decides to leave.

Yet you're worth it to me.
What's it worth to you to love me properly?
As I demonstrate what I need
with instructions written clearly,
will you take the time to read
or toss them aside and start improvising?

I'm not scared to let you in.
I'm careful.

Beyond ready to put the shield down.
My arms are tired and muscles exhausted.
So can I trust you?
Can I put trust in your care to
love me as much as God does?
You haven't asked me once how I receive love
or what parts need extra caressing.
You've never inquired why you only ever see me smile
and where I retreat to when
my sadness comes out for a little while.

Investigate me
and extrapolate the intricacies
of where you can help me build
when you see where I need
to grow and where I lack.
Are you capable of that?

I study you.
I've taken careful examination
of where you're strong
and where you're bruised
to love you in the right places
and gently nurse your wounds.
I listen to your cosmic tunes.
When I move into your heart,
I make it a home.
Know that you're never alone.

I'm not scared to let you in.
I'm conscientious.

Hyper-aware that I'm malleable and delicate
as a powerful ocean is ubiquitous.
Am I silly for feeling like I need you most times?
When I want to share some good news
or vocalize what's on my mind.
Is it ridiculous that I make my life
readily available for you to fold into
like Archangel Metatron's cube?

I always want you.
No matter what I'm going through,
your happiness and love is in my prayers too.
Every night I ask God
and tell the angels to let me dream of you
so we can be metaphysically bound.

Do I sound absurd for having the urge to
splurge on multilayered words?
Not a language on this earth
has enough verbs to adequately articulate
the magnitude of desire to ventilate my heart.

So, I'm opening the door now...
Remove your shoes upon entry
with this clary sage cleanse.
I'm letting you in...
Prove to me it's my best decision.

Organic

He has a love like fruit.
Like coconut water
which quenches the deepest thirst.
Righteously, he's got my skin glowing.
Love like a citrus smoothie
with double ginger;
energetic and extra spicy
with a few papaya seeds.
His love is cleansing.
Love like maple syrup
and blueberry preserves
spread on a hot stack of flapjacks.
His love glides.
And I like him Americano style.
Black coffee no sugar no cream; surplus caffeine.
Not for the weak & just right for my team.
Hay dios mío, I'm in love with his intensity.
Love like almond butter and açaí.
Antioxidants to free me
of all the radicals I've been ingesting.
His love heals.
Love like bananas;
fresh and frozen too.
Our connection on a slow blend; nice and thick.
His love is filling.
Love like apples & grapes
when I need a little wine and dine
to arouse my mind.
Pour a bit of red as I kiss his head.
His love makes me lush.
Love like passion fruit and honeydew
once Ramadan comes to close.
Tastes like spring and new beginnings.
His love is refreshing.
A love like his unequivocally is
the ripest fruit I've ever tasted.

By DesigN

Regarding
the one thing you do
compared to nothing else-
What is there to prove?

So lean back
while I straddle your lap
in the warmth of a west coast day,
periwinkle blue lingerie.
Read books with me all day.

Just breathe.
Inhaling eucalyptus aromatherapy,
a conscientious chi.
Time to study the aftermath of a Love Jones
hit hard yet so effortlessly.
Cursive and calligraphy-
pages covered by unique designs
of strokes specified
so neat, the ink
traces back a few miles.

A "je ne sais quoi"...
Whatever you're doing, keep doing it.
Happiness looks handsome on you.

if you're sure

You don't always make it apparent.
The magnitude of your love.
Consistency is not consistently
communicated creatively through your cranium
or the cage your heart still sleeps in.

Guessing becomes taxing to my heart;
I'm the infinity pool that never runs dry.
I don't flow "sometimes".
Yet it's only some times that I feel you.

I'm a deep lover.
Emotionally expensive,
spiritually luxury,
cosmically upper echelon.
Reserved for the most exquisite
into my orbit.
So be cognizant of my disposition;
understand the reason and listen.
It's imperative I ascertain the risk of giving more
when you tell me you love me
and I ask you

if you're sure.

Un-Complex

I remember it used to hurt when you left.
But you've left so many times that I'm numb to it now
and that numbness has turned into superhuman strength.
I can punch through brick and not feel my bones ache-
really a power I've always had.
I sat it on the shelf wanting to be soft for you-
give you chances you didn't deserve
even in your growing pains.
You've made the process of letting you go easy;
it's not me, it's you.
I held on to be patient with and teach you
that a true goddess can recognize
when you're working on changing for the better.
But what's love to a snake that would bite its own tail
when it feels like it's being attacked?
It's not like you were my emperor,
but a trodden soul that called to me who desired love.
I loved you without judgment.
You boot strapped old patterns and bad habits;
it's unfortunate you have to go now.
I've written enough poems about you.
Because not everyone who enters my Love Temple
has earned the rights to see it through.

Are You Up For The Challenge?

Tell me you love me
without saying "I love you".
Of course, I want those words too,
but I'd like you
to get creative & I'm sure you can do it.
Ascertain my comprehension of your intention.
Without question, a 3 syllable truth.
Learn all you can,
stand in strong command,
be resourceful & give it good cadence.
Tell me you love me
without saying "I love you".
Put parts of me in everything you create.
What connects U & S is T-
time between us;
chronologically, we're the perfect solution.
After all is said (but never done),
by the time "I love you" comes,
I'll know it's coming straight from your soul.

Lack

It's the lack of passion in sex
The absence of sacredness
That makes it just a bunch of senseless fucking

Pleasure

What I've learned about an orgasm,
is that it's spiritual.
And while a climax that makes me shout to rooftops
when you hit the g spot is purely physical,
an orgasm shared is tentatively lyrical.

An orgasm can be shared without penetration.
A back breaking, soul shaking, kundalini activation
reaches cosmic zenith when two spirits
leave bodies to dance in 5D incantation-
iridescent geometric da Vinci code shaping.
My love, that's an orgasm.

And baby, I see it in your eyes.
You've never had a real orgasm yet.
You like how she's slippery when wet; that's basic sex.
A simple climax test.
Feeling an alkaline yoni is new for you too.
No shame boo;
it's exciting when your senses are heightened.
A good Ph = Portal of harmony balance.
Not acidic. Alkaline for your magic stick.
Feels incredible and pleasurable,
sure to plea that you please for good measure.

Climbing to the max is great-
like Mt. Everest's apex changing our breath rate.
But real orgasmic nature stimulates supernovas,
full 5 point star reverse engineering.
It's a ceremony of inverted alpha helices rotating in space
until we reach golden ratio state.

Bodies dissolve past skin and bone.
Only nerve endings exist
and traces linger of pheromones.
The two don't pair alone.
Binding ritual shown-
suprachiasmtic nuclei sharing.

Synced nights, infused days... in a daze work.
We're love prone.

Knowing an orgasm is purely spiritual,
you be my first, I'll be your first...
let's make a miracle.

Just Desserts

I'm brown sugar cinnamon spice
glazed on hot peaches.
Take spoonfuls of my love,
curve your craving for my sweetness.

Each bite is everything you like
while we skate over marvelous ideas.
The the fire we create has been turned up to the Max...
well so you can know the Keys to this feature
is that Alicia was my teacher-
& our souls already connecting
in the motion picture of our next lives.

I see those smiles you make as I feed you cheesecake.
Just one kiss strawberry glossed on my lips...

You deserve to be honoured with praise.
A "thank you" for not giving up on your hardest days
so God could bring you right to me.
Shall we feast on the treats I prepared?
Let's celebrate, every moment lasts forever;
no week ends.
Float on my elegance
and you'll swim without sinking- a buoyant being.

To shower you with my femininity,
sweeter than butter pecan.
My gift to you, and we can
keep going through every cycle of the moon.
I'm your Oshun.

It's Love Related

It's love related
and I can't negate the time it's taking,
yet time is not linear
– it revolves around me.
So delicately, we build.
We pray together when nights are still;
a pillar of our protected connection.
I own the copyrights to your love,
trademarks to your heart,
patents to the recipe
– it's all mine.

It's love related

so I must learn your darkness
where we disagree and debate,
pouring in love and shakes from earthquakes.
I could never love you less, only more.
No matter where you are in life,
whether cloudy or clear night, moonshines
– I send sterling kisses through moonlight.
I imprint lips of mahogany tint on your soul.

My silver to your gold.

Garden

Without proper care,
a garden becomes overgrown
and overflown with weeds
that put its natural beauty in a chokehold.
Closed gate to its potential.
Ivy covers the locks.

That doesn't make the garden any less amazing.
That doesn't mean it's worth hating
because of the space it's taking.
Let an angel lend a hand.

You're a garden too.
Just need some tending to.
Let me go grab my tools.

My love pulls weeds and
tills to soil for fresh seeds that
only require a little tlc
to bud beautifully.

Make similes of your smiles and similarly
with "I love you" while birds sing-
all of nature's r&b jams.

Be You

You just need to be seen.
You only want to be heard.
For the one you are inside
without any flashy words.

Your "friends" would respect you more
if you met your end
so they could wear you on a t-shirt.
They see how bad you want to change
and kick your dreams down until you go insane.
That way, you'll never grow greater than them.

Your girl loves you less each time you express
the weight that's on your heart.
Out here gazing into the eyes of a serpent,
trying to impress her
while enduring the pressure
of living a double life.

And I see you king, a great god.
I'm your friend, your queen,
your love messenger.
With me, you can just be.
Allow me to journey through your eyes,
foreheads pressed
and just rub your shoulders for a sec.
I'm talking to your greatest asset.
Your beautiful soul,
I hold with so much respect.

Delivery

You're adding more weight to the scale
to make it look like
there's more treats in your package,
but you're really just piling on extra baggage.
You've taken those wounded memories
and self sabotaging antics
out of storage then sent it all to me
so you can rid yourself of storage fees;
expedited delivery.
Asking me to sort through and store it for free.
But at what cost to me?
We share commonalities
yet I can't fathom your rationality;
believing I'd ever keep a surplus inventory
of selves you'd rather run from than face.

I don't come to you with a heavy load.
Only a small envelope of imperfections- mail worth opening.
I send my spirit healed.
I packed light
so you don't have to pay the hefty price.
No extra shipping and handling,
or stress from back tracking a parcel on delay.
Little by little, brought it all to surface
so I could repair and repurpose
everything I almost let break me.

Immensely, intensely, I want to love you
and I feel how much I'm needed but your heart's messy;
mind is too cluttered to receive it.

Because, right away, I would send my love
and Amazon prime
couldn't get it there quick enough.
Only nano light waves
can transport such a bundle.
Disclaimer: it's fragile, don't stumble.
My love is precious cargo.

Someday you'll give without taking,
pour without dumping,
hold without shaking.
Excuse me, your item is not even exchange.
I sent love. I got delivered pain.
"Return To Sender".
There's nothing I gain from
having this in my name.

Skinside

The birds sent me messages
of what you see in your dreams,
how you're always thinking of me.

I'm delighted,
I must say,
to partake in my spirit's extracurricular activities.
A happy place to be.

I want to step inside your house,
just take a visit.
Take a peek inside your home
and see how your soul is living.
Only a short minute.

Your inner child is still a bit timid;
here's a cup of chamomile lavender tea
to calm your nerves and bring you closer to me.

Now that I'm in,
show me the foundation;
are you strong and ready to rumble
or made of sticks that can easily crumble?

What's the 411?
The message I got from the birds was cute,
but walk me inside your skin
so I can see the real you.

Verde Día

What's my name?
That's not important;
Tonight I'm whoever you say.
Right now I just need you come with me
So that I can have you my way.
From sage to emerald,
Every shade dripping from my pores.
Heart chakra, love galore-
I just gotta love some more.

And I choose you.
Do you agree, arbitrarily
To step into my room
Underneath full moon
And succumb to righteous pleasure?

No time can measure
Or storm can weather
An experience better;
A covalent bond that can never be severed.

How do you write "love"
In my heart?
With your smiles and your questions.
We know how to speak the same language;
That makes me happy.

I think we need to run
Away with the clouds
And focus on spelling "love"
With the elements.
Do you know how to swim?
Because we will be swimming through life
Until time stops.

¿Cuál es mi nombre?
Eso no es importante;
Esta noche soy quien tú digas.
Ahora sólo necesito que vengas conmigo
Para poder tenerte a mi manera.
De salvia a esmeralda
Cada tono gotea de mis poros
Chakra del corazón, amor en abundancia-
Solo me queda amar un poco mas.

Y yo te elijo.
¿Estás de acuerdo, arbitrariamente
Para entrar a mi habtitación
Debajo de la luna llena
¿Y sucumbir al placer correcto?

Ningún tiempo puede medir
O tormenta puede capear
Una mejor experiencia;
Un enlace covalente que nunca se puede romper.

¿Cómo se escribe "amor"
En mi corazón?
Con tus sonrisas y tus preguntas.
Sabemos hablar las mismas idiomas;
Eso me hace feliz.

Creo que necesitamos huye
Con las nubes
y concéntrate en deletrear "amor"
Con los elementos.
Sabes nadar?
Porque nadaremos por la vida
Hasta que el tiempo se detenga.

Build

I wanna break you,
But gently
Tear down
Your cracked walls
Built on pain
Turn them
To dust
And build you
Up again

Watch them crumble
I only want
To see you,
Not who
You had to be
And build
It new
Gently,
I wanna break you

A Butterfly Beacon

There was a version of me accustomed
to the wrath of lightning gods-
allowing each strike to burn holes in my chest
and send my metaphysical love
into cardiac arrest.

Once upon a time,
it was dangerous for me
to talk so soft and be so sweet.

The ravaged ones only knew how to exist precariously
with blank stare & cold vicious grin
where a soul is supposed to be.

A butterfly has no business in a blizzard.
So I had to change form for survival
and almost got locked in the armor.

But you found my being.
Ready to protect this butterfly
from bitter winds and storms.

Now, even on the foggiest of nights,
my beacon glows from the lighthouse;
it led you straight to my heart
with tranquil waters instead of raging seas.

My calm currents currently curate
a quiet course for you to navigate
the path where our entire being courageously relates.

Dame tu corazón
so I know where you are
and you'll always feel home.

As I sing the song between us two,
waiting in my butterfly garden,
this poetry flowing over me
frolicking through silk robes
and satin sheets.

Love in linguistics
and in the language that doesn't speak.
This is more than a love story.
It's me open to you
since you're open to see.

Double Direction

If you really are
in the cycle of my love,
you'd read that the price of entry
is wearing your soul on your sleeve
for me to assess
if you're worthy of seeing
what's under my dress.

Did you study my love bible?
My ancient literature is a genius test
to know if you've truly learned.
The lines you recite aren't quite mine.
Your library is full: broken words
and ripped pages of what girl minds
pieced together from misinformed shreds.
Inherently useless texts.

I need you to need my mind so much
that this becomes a centripetal force love-
the mass and exponential direction
of our souls growing
cannot be separated
by the distance of our bodies.

Only then, can we eminently touch.
Read my love scripture once more;
memorize it to the core
and prepare thine self for
millennia of what's in store.

Traveller

You're part of everything
that means anything to me.
For you, I'm forever in heart's reach.
With long distance relationships:
voyages, excursions,
explorations, and expeditions...
great ships are meant to travel long distances.
That's where the treasure is.

What Happens In 4

Carpe diem, seize the day.
No more professors, just profess to her
how light you'll make her mind.

You chose her and she chose you
underneath the diamonds and tattoos.
Mix her knowledge and your smarts.
Create a better point of view
College boys ain't hitting;
she wanna build something new.

Right after exams, glasses come off.
She'll be at your show
to teach you what she learned,
backstage, lights low.
A really good college girl
who only wants you to know
how she likes to get, as above so below.

Just got her degree now turn her up 500°
Dig deep, slowly, yes please.
All the right fun a college girl needs.

Graduated with honours,
she's an honorable mention.
8 semesters later, help her relieve the tension.
She knows you're more gentle than you put on;
she really has more fun when college is done & gone.
Now what's next wild boy?
What type of fun is there to get on?

2099

I want to learn the pattern of your heartbeat
and sing to it,
covering you with a love like oxygen.
Everywhere.
And serenade you with my linguistics.

I've always believed in miracles and you're example 2099
of how life just gets better with time.

And it feels like a taste I can hear when I see it.
Can you guess what this savoury sensation is?
It just might be love
because you make it so easy to love you.
Even if it got difficult, I'd still choose you.

The mere sound of you
saying my name is good for my soul.
It glimmers and glows.
All that glitters really is gold.
You shine my silver ten fold.
What's a god to a goddess foretold?

As I'm remembering your skin on my skin,
you know exactly what you did.
Now I count the moments
until I see you again.
My intuition tells me when I'm on your heart
or when I dance inside your cognition and lately,
my entire being has felt like: woah.

West

Little flame from the west is the last one left.
And that's precisely where you are in relation to me.
Direct my body westward and I feel it in my chest –
confirmation of your love for me.
Only the strong survive. Our worlds collide.
Demonstrate the level of great it gets with you in it.
Put me deeper in yours
so I can pour into you like I really yearn to.
I told the universe I'd like an artist to be with me –
who understands & innerstands my language
and will immortalize my being.
And here you are.
By third contact, we had a contract
to connect with much respect,
Alhamdullilah.

Set

As the sun sets,
And day rests,
My heart eases,
And spirit is blessed.
The colours & hues,
Creatively move,
While I think of you.
Strawberry sun,
As day is done,
We are one,
My love, let's run.

Firefighter

That fire in you refused to be a flame that died.
You had to burn everything within you and around you
to rebuild a new flame inside.

You can warm your people now
instead of burning them.
Use that fire for light instead of hurting them.
You saved yourself from your own wildfire.
Your soul is home now
and the flame is a new nighttime ride.

You had to turn yourself to ashes;
make it all a black soot
at the bottom of your foot
that you now use as ink for new tribal marks.
Fire is God, who gave us the sun –
our personal fire abroad.

I'll always love the flame on my skin
that darkens my melanin;
the perfect harmony.

See, you just needed The Universe
to teach you.
That fire in you refused to be a flame that died.
So grateful to have fire by my side.
A colour combination to show, never to hide.

The Last Discovery

Every part of me is meant for you.
You're the only one strong enough,
patient enough,
gentle enough to make it through
– take your time now.

Every part of me is meant for you.
The one who learned how to read thim slick girls,
I mean, slim thick curves –
or whatever Fabolus & Jeremih said.

Every part of me is meant for you
to take this little waist
into contorted proportions
of cosmically metamorphic shapes.

Every part of me is meant for you;
to be your watermelon and hydrate too.
You know, I have a lot in common with that fruit:
1. we share the same stretch marks
2. we have that sweet pink inside
meant to be your most energetic food.

The perfect amount to keep you focused in full;
every part of me is meant for you.
Body and soul
– just how Anita Baker sang it.
As long as your heart is open to me,
every part of me is ready.

A Wizard Making It Disappear

Please me,
my light in my dark sides,
my left and my right thighs,
but don't beat it like a drum,
let me show you what to do it like.

Like your decoding an ancient Anunnaki scroll,
gentle and attentive
to the microcosmic life living
and loving on 150 trillion
smiling cells of me.

Do it like an orchestra plays
– using your bow
back and forth in my
…excuse me…
on my violin.

The higher my note,
the longer you stroke
972 Hz
my shining crown chakra shows.

And just do it like
your light energy wants to dissipate
the entropy in the walls.

Please me,
my light and my dark sides,
my left and my right thighs,
but don't beat it like a drum,
let me show you what to do it like.

Please my primal tribal instincts.
Show me why
you should be the chief of the lot.
Let my spirit guides tell me
if I should submit on the spot.

Pleasing to Mother Nature,
your green thumb
protecting the fortress proudly.
Nature's glory?
Yeah you get some.

And please
I ask you,
I'll spell it out if I have to,
to stay deep in this ether of astronaut knowledge
so the universal oneness
can have a good story to hear
when it's time to pay homage.

Shakes

It just begins to piss me off
thinking about the people
who've done you wrong, imagining the times
when having someone like you in my life
would've been that single log
floating in the river I can grab on to when I'm about to be
swept under by unforgiving currents.
You've helped too many people
too comfortable hurting you.
Your heart is black and blue
instead of its rich burgundy hues.
Exceeding empathy; I got bruises too.

And I just cannot believe
they were all so careless with you.
Putting me in position
to overuse my actions to prove what you can do for me
is not only why I love you.
Extra delicate with your heart
because you came to me so injured.
So used to people using you that it confuses you why
I don't want anything from you.
Perhaps an array of unfamiliar pieces.
Quite frankly, I'm appalled.

And then my hands start to shake-
sending signals to The Most High;
a message request he can answer best:
"how does one fall so short of such a blessing?"

Tears well up in my eyes
noticing how nervous life has made you.
Head spinning at identical crossroads.
Wondering if giving selflessly again
would be to your detriment.
I'm over qualified to care for your heart-
my field of expertise.
Most sacred treasure.
There's nothing you have to do alone again.

CHAPTER 2:
APPROACHING ME

Poet

I'm a poet, of course I write until my hand hurts.
Until my pen becomes the explorer
of uncharted territory,
searching jungles of synapses for new species.
Joints connecting my metacarpals stiffen,
preparing to bleed into the wet ink.
Fingertips want to run
while my pen tip begs them to stay.
Nothing can pry me away from these words.
Until I think myself dizzy.
Yet unable to faint.
Unwilling to disentangle from my instrument.
Until my lips go numb
from plosives and sibilance
sneaking and exploding through
drifts of silence;
begging only makes us go longer.
And it hurts so good.
Burns so boldly.
But what is pain to the poet?
Continuing through the pool of profusion
in sonorous forevers.
Gazing upon blistering fingers
which articulate a sound uncommon to man.
A poet knows no bounds.

Course of Action

My name IS Mahogany.
I don't wear it to sound cute.
I am from the stars.
Resting on the moon.
Traveling through galaxies.
Visiting earth a time or two.

I am a healer; I'm a heart healer.
Life is my master- granted as a gift
for me to keep my promise
in exchange for this existence.

One heart at a time.
To do that, I use my mind.
My head is big and small, but fine- it's universe shaped.
Filled with wisdom and reminders of
god's incredible creations.

But a few rules come with living in this society;
Here's the set:
#1: never let them see me sweat
#2: don't lose self tryna chase a check
#3: I have the playing cards, so conceal the full deck

Use my gifts to heal my soul and help my people,
Like rule three, the methodology is quiet as kept.
Uphold honour and respect.
With the sheep, I protect.

My whole life I've waited for this moment.
More can be better, but what I've been given is golden.
Gorgeous pieces I'm molding.

Comparison of old memories
to new vision helps me be where I am.
I'm grateful for it since I was once
buried the wrong mind.
Pressure placed on me, now it's show time.
Lotus from the roots, gotta reveal mine.

I love the way sun shines through clouds
in radiant beams when I take the time to
look up while everyone else faces
forward or down.

And with my chin up to the sky,
appreciating Earth's beauty,
I say this:
"I'm a messenger; God use me"

There's too much power in words
to use them deceptively, dumbly, or disrespectfully.
That's a storm inside unquiet,
Mobbing Deep inside my mind.
So I'm careful with mine
while The Universe keeps checking me.

Don't speak unless what's said is
kind and/or necessary.
With God's plan for me,
all of it is love's necessity.

While navigating this map,
I'll continue to pray and say Asé
because so it is;
myself and all those I'm meant to save.

PTO

Excuse me...
Would you mind if I took a little PTO
to gather myself?
Mind you, I've always been mindful
of the work I put in
and learning from the school of hard knocks
while balancing this job
is quite demanding.
I could really use a break.
I've never missed a day and always stay late.
My thoughts are on speed dial for you.
Doing my best to sound polite
because I've requested my whole life
and still been denied-
I'm not asking this time.
You owe me.
During my hiatus, I'll take my payments in sanity.
I'm going on extended vacation.
Undoing, unwinding, erasing
the smears, stains, and blurbs clouding my view
from living in my truth.
You really are piece of work.
Don't call my brain asking
to relive the fragments of life learned
and reminiscing on the times we didn't have.
I have too much value
to waste life letting you intrude.

Body of Art

In awe and amazement of her temple.
A vibrantly etheric spirit
wrapped up in beautiful casing.
Even rain thanks the clouds
for the privilege of touching her body and face.
Every garment draped
over her body gives God thanks-
to share a short moment
of keeping her treasures secret.

Simply adorn the placement of her waist.
Every subtle curve in the right place
to rest your head on
and cleanse your troubles away.
Her statuesque shape,
a uniquely rare vase crafted by the same hands
who made the ocean part ways.

She saunters and sways in stilettos
with legs long like rivers:
The Nile and Euphrates.
Powerful and bold... oh the mysteries they hold.
Smoothness from the physical and as gentle as her touch.
Delicate and such,
them type ladies are the slickest explorers.

She maintains the gifted avatar by Universe's grace;
She has everything in perfect proportions.
Correct measurements for perfect cake.

A blessing never to disguise or hide.
Put offerings on her altar
because that amount of pulchritude has no price.
Only godly eyes can recognize.

Almighty

Goodness! Goddess, rule this   all in.
Moonstruck, falling   in love with me tonight.

Get a good whiff, a good scent
of this godd-ess
this god-(ess)ence;
a flash of love through past/present
to have for all your life.

And I Do Grow

And I do grow.
They just keep stepping on the petals
so the growth struggles to show.
But the roots run deep.
A light year's experience
coursing through dark matter.
And I do grow,
but they have a twisting need
to see the same picture
through a distorted lens
of fallen pieces.
Tainted eyes matter not
because I do grow.
Scorched leaves and dried petals
always disintegrate with due time;
all that will be left is what's new.

Taking Over

Have a seat with me.
Let's sit and contemplate the past on repeat, shall we?
And piece together worst case scenarios-
preparing for things that haven't happened yet
so you're ready for anything.
I'm promise I'm only helping.
Helping you navigate this cruel world
and be overly cautious about what you do and say;
helping you remember you can't have it your way
because everything is subject to change.

I have an unnatural attachment to you-
an obsessive compulsive addiction
to be where I don't fit in,
yet I always feel better when I'm the center of attention.
I want you to be happy but not too happy,
just enough to wake up each day
and let me lead because it hurts
when you feel happier without me...

While you try to learn your shadows,
I'd rather you fight our battles-
because how could you ever be over me?
You're over thinking?
No, you're overthinking about overthinking
and it's right back to me, me, me; just how it should be.

I like to make your thoughts scatter
and drift in every direction.
I like to interrupt your prayers
and break your meditation.
I like you unfocused on living
so I can be the center of attention.

I love feeling needed
and it pains me to know how powerful you'd be
by breaking free of my misery;
your company is just too sweet.

I enjoy making you squirm
while filling your mind with ludicrous distractions
so you don't take action.
It makes me calm to see you frantic.
If I can keep making you feel inadequate,
we can stay in this comforting spot of analysis paralysis.
This is no relationship, but a relation-island.
Ships get to move, but I like us stagnant and silent.
More time I get to grow.

By depleting you
of everything that makes you special,
eventually you'll stop trying to be free
and just let me take over this host.
You should be thanking me;
my gift to you is this syndrome called Stockholm.
You love being controlled.

You need me gone to live life.
I need to keep you for me to multiply.
A devious parasite.
It's either you or me;
so I'll keep controlling your thoughts
by living rent free in your mind
if it means I get to survive.

Deus Ex Machina

Deus Ex Machina (I've always been)
planted in a certain place to stir it up and change.

Placed in peoples lives at God's perfect moment
when they feel all is hopeless,
to resolve the confusion.

And I've always been –
a god from a machine
(the textbook definition
of what Deus Ex Machina means),
but my machine is LIFE.

The same way AI
has dropped down into commoners' lives,
but isn't actually new to GI (Galactic Intelligent) minds.

A machine turning the LLM
from Large Language Model
into Love Language Model
– universally placed to decode
the unsolvable problems living in their hearts.

Out of thin air, from nowhere,
I share messages from where spirits thrive.
A messenger from all spirit sides.
And light away for them.

Speed Dial

No need to keep my contact list long.
Even if I did,
I'd have no one to call.

Giver's Dilemma

Because if I could, I truly would.
In every moment, I would be there:
giving, lending, and showing.

More abundance in a past
that no longer exists
would have just given me more access
to assist
and backtest
the formula of what not to do
when people aren't equally as good to you.

Some have it to give over 100x
and wouldn't share a dime.
But not me;
possibly a burden of mine and that's fine.

Maybe God purposely put me on a limit
for a short while
so I could learn not to overexert
to those who choose to be selfish, angry, or hurt.

It all makes sense now.
Forced to be stationary
so I could slow down and see:
"only give to those who earn the giving"
Because if I could've, truly would've.

What's it like
to care about everything too much?

Red Alert

Have you ever watched your soul
leave your body in mid consciousness?
Looking at your body animate
on the other side of glass doors
– amazed at how you still haven't dropped to the floor?
Well I have
– now that's really a scary story.
I watched myself from both lenses
– my warning call.
My wake up message…
that next time could be permanent;
Either live a full life or don't exist at all.

Led By God

In human minds,
the word "submission" can be triggering.
It's thought of as giving your power away.
But I say,
it's a giving way to innerstand
how a piece becomes part of the whole.

Mission embarks a voyage to send messages
across multidimensional channels,
so sub-mission is a sharper frequency channel
sending tighter messages one shouldn't miss:
a mission within a mission.
Don't sleep on the vision.

Yet never am I willing to acquiesce to mediocrity.
You're not allowed to ask me to let you lead
if you're lead by the absence of thoughts
in a caveman's head.

But instead you must be moved by God.
To where if a hurricane tries to spin the block on you,
you stand firm and unshaken until God says move.
That's a man I can submit to.

You respect me respecting you.
Olodumare guides our developmental moves.
We walk together in our spirit guides' shoes.

Kneeling before The Most High
is what I already do every day anyway,
so he who kneels with me
is one I'll nestle with femininity willingly.

In the eyes and hands of equidistant power,
I profess my servitude to the vision.

Not to mention,
we operate this human experience
in similar intention.

You calculate your choices by listening to Allah
with guidance from His messengers,
signs, natural orders...
that's man I can trust.
One who honours God, honours me.
It's cosmic mathematics-
a self fulfilling prophecy.

When a man leads properly,
a woman will submit naturally.
I submit my will to the Universal Cosmic Order-
ways appointed. No exceptions.
Jah bless
and the rest is already written.

Can I Still Wish

I wish I may I wish I might
have this wish I wish tonight.
Wishes spoke in screeches
get muffled with love
from a planet light years away.
If this wish is one I may have tonight,
carry me into orbit with Orion's light.

Happy Tears

I have moments when I think about my emperor
and who he will be, how he'll come to me,
and where he is now.
What stage of life is he in? Is he happy?
When is the last time he's been loved?
Is he praying to find me yet?
Does he think about what my love will be like?
Has he become anointed by The Universe
to have earned my love now?
Or must we both stay patient?

I have moments when I envision his touch
and how our hands will interlock...
what his scent will be like
embedded in my mind
and the culmination of sensations I'll get
when he looks at me with those eyes.

In each of those moments,
I can feel him searching for me-
waiting for the grandfather clocks to align
so we can find
one another.
Enthusiastically exuberant.

In each of those moments,
I pray for him. I pray he is safe.
I pray he is loved.
I pray that his wisdom precedes his years.
And I welcome him.

Mother

It's all my mother's fault.
She set my expectations for love so high,
I still believe my heart can fly.
She did this to me.
Well past 10,000 hours
of masterfully training my soul.
I promised her to never settle for less.
My mother made me this way.
Protected every part of the adolescent me
to the best of her abilities
so I could learn differently.
Regardless of a few emotional abrasions,
I'm indebted to her raising.
She chose to keep my fire hot.
It's all on her.
A love unique.
And it's alright with me.

On A Mission

Let me listen
I'm on a mission

Take in my essence when I talk
No stressin'
Let no stress in

Soul gets soggy when I sulk

Fear is dead
Worry gone
Since me and death
Went on a tightrope walk

Didn't have to die
To know that side

Now I see past faults

Life is my new gas pack
Super high off that

Still every once in a blue
When I like to slow cruise
I'll buy a lil za
and get zooted on the back end too

But back to the point....

For a lot of suns and moons
I've been tapped in
Needed a transformation
Before I could MAKE life happen

Stayed in the dark
Until my headlights got fixed
And started flashing

Because how you drive the whip at night
With 5% tint, no lights,
And dark ass sunglasses?

Oh no... you're DEFINITELY crashing!

And that was me for a while
On a road of shenanigans
Still tryna claim it an accident

Bumping into other cars
with the same story,
Excuse time!
Let me get heavy with my accent

"No habla inglés
Lo siento
Yo no sé!
Necesito salir rápido"
Let me just go where it's safe

That was never okay

So with myself I stayed
Until I learned the true way

In harmony with death and life
Now my six principles

Are all calm as night and clear as day

All Night

All night, some nights
I turn and I toss
over the profit and cost
of the rights I've wronged
and blessings I lost.

Acceptance of that which was never truly mine
can be the hardest at times
since always in my mind
I wonder, "why me?"
"How exactly did I get to this point?".

And the truth is
as long as there's and angel,
there's a chance;
Worry not- because stillness of night
is exactly where the fountain of youth lives.

Heart first, I jump into
the pool of my thoughts
wading in the tide of moonlight-
waiting til sunrise to show the angels
how many fruits of labour I bought.

Yet for now, I lay here;
patiently I stay
until profit pays
knowing with each night,
I may not get all day.

Approaching

There's a pressure and a weight
of who I'm supposed to be
controlling me
and I'm compelled to perform righteously.
Compassionately, I approach.
Not too prideful to ask for help but every time I knelt,
God said it's only me and him.
I always come through when I'm needed,
but I haven't caught a break yet;
maybe my arms aren't open in the right places still.
The Most High watches me proudly as I move soundly –
never breaking down where they can see,
yet my chest stays pounding.
I must be calm in my frustrations
through patience and meditation –
taking control where I can.
No more feeling helpless,
just help me and help less
until I can help more for them and be help full to me.
If what I want must wait,
I'll study to the very day
and be ready for what I'm called to do.
Asé

I Thank The Universe

And my story is still being written,
for now I share a piece.
All glory be for what I'm learning.
One day the memoir shall be ready.
Found more love in my soul
than I've ever given myself credit for – worldwide.

All praises to The Most High.
For everything I have and what I'm working to create,
I live the Zen Tao Ma'at way;
my peace no one can ever take.

My love is for those who need it,
cultivated and seeded
given to me by The Universal Spirit.
I can hear the angels cheering,
and God catching me when I jump or feel defeated.

The one and only, a supreme goddess,
yet she remains modest.
Only to speak truth and live a life that's honest
to one day relay what she learned while in the body.

With transcendent consciousness,
teach my youth prosperity;
help them be gracious adults
from becoming immaculate kids.
Show them how passion frees the mind to a purpose shift.
Love is what my purpose is.

Prophetic for me to uphold; create from speaking poetry.
My ancestors and spirit guides
have so much more to show me.
All praises and all glory.

Translation

English Version:
"I'm exhausted"

Poetry Translation:
"The weight of trying to make meaning of this life
has anchored me to a place which my arms have become limp.
No longer can I lift"

English Version:
"I don't know"

Poetry Translation:
"If clarity was at the tip of my nose,
my clouded vision
would prevent my comprehension"

English Version:
"No"

Poetry Translation:
"Acquiescence danced on the rim of my quivering lip,
but sound fell faint
and I knew there was only one answer"

Wat(her)

Always in flow.
I am water.
Waves grow.
Also from roots.
High tides show.
Pray deeply.
Relinquish control.

Great In Good Taste

Inside of me, is some insanity.
It takes a lot to overstand me and choose to stand with me.
This predilection of melanin is an acquired taste
for a refined palate.
I'm dusted in gold flakes.

I'm an archetype of wife betrothed to the very gods
who once ruled our empires.

I'm obliged to tie solely to a great man:
artist, revolutionary, inventor, polymath
with an immaculate mind, pure heart, and strong stance.
Only I can see into him the way no one else can.

I like them misunderstood by the world-
a greatness so few can inhale and intake but I'm ye-ye,
come lay upon thee if he wanna go to heaven.

I'm his eyes and ears when needed-
assigned directly to his spirit,
I hold his heart with no fears.

Audacious, tenacious, (tender when I need him)
vivacious, ferocious, a declarative statement.
He needs a woman who doesn't
pressure him into normality,
instead challenges his greatness.

To think more, to love more.
Be more than ever before.
That wild tumultuous locomotive gets me going.

Never will he ever
spend a lifetime
or phone a life line
down a rusty pipeline
of putrid personalities,
translating his soul
to low vibrating mush minded trolls.

A mediocre chick
is a superior man's greatest downfall.
Little baby chicken head
bumbling around with a one track mind
and can't even fly-
unable to see her man is a phoenix.
Nothing she offers but noisy screeches.
He must know he deserves more.

A supreme feminine
is a man's greatest gift
next to his soul-
to keep him on track of ascension.

Should he not be in the position
to be the best of the best,
walk past me and give it a rest.
Don't even come my way.

If he is though, let's chat.
I have a lot to say.

Challenging

Write for me
rightfully
insightfully
I can be
righteously
inquiring
perfect timing
with the pen.
All it can be
but all it's not
time been spent
my freedom bought
weighed on me
like bouldered knots
but no one makes it look better.
To lead in love
is an honour
a duty be stowed upon her
earned my place among the stars
with this pressure
I make amends.
It's like this pen has a mind of its own
traveling through my mind
to scribe the lessons it's been shown.
Let it wander and travel
just to find it next to Basquiat's home.

Keeper No Keeping

There's something about liking a man
you know can't be kept.
Frolicking in the graveyard turns exciting.
You're an adrenaline junkie.
Willingly sharing loads of love with someone who
prefers to break bread with sharks and demons.
To a man you recognize as prone to mistreating.

Arms just shy of enough to keep him at length
so little by little, fondness grows.
You like him more.
The IK in **li**k**e** tells you:
"I KNOW what I'm doing"
But you don't
and the IK gets replaced with OV.
It's OV
when his l**ov**e
slowly
sends your heart to the ER.
It's **over**. You OD'ed accidentally.
No turning back.

No one wants to be damaged.
But baby girl, the consequences of just being friends
and making up benefits
will leave more questions than answers.
Chaos is sign of deep wounds.

Lack of reciprocity is probably diabolically
starving your heart's autonomy.
It wants to beat easy, breathe freely.
Love is not a drug to be hooked on or needy.
What is yours will be, and maybe it's not him.

Gotta Count For Something

Thumbed through 52 weeks every year
like chapters I skimmed in college for my essays.
"I got the important parts", I told tell myself.
But I could only remember 7 lines
out of 365 pages in my life.
Thought I found the cheat code.
Had my mind fabricate an effort
I wasn't truly ready to make.

Let the days on my bookshelf collect dust,
and I wasn't trying to give up.
Yet each layer of debris piled on
right in between a rock and the place I got stuck.

The formula for finesse isn't the same one for success;
the harder I tried to win, the further I would regress.
Everything was so far that nothing felt best.

Beginning at the last line and racing to the start.
They said speed was the compliment to success
only to be as fair as paying extra fees for bounced checks.
But even then, I couldn't settle for less.

Was a tell tale heart, a tell tale sign.
Old ways I had to resign to divinely navigate
the labyrinth of existence with life.
No more crying at the evil force burying my efforts
underneath creaky floor boards.

It was always me
battling choice versus mahogany-
A sad one on one
with no outcome promising.

I wrote suicide notes
to my higher self in the dark,
slipping elevation through the cracks
and both hands tied behind my back.

Stayed bound in the sorrows
I imprisoned myself in thinking
"it's gotta count for something"
until I learned to let me win.

Can't have what I want.
Only get what I am.
Blessings will run til I become,
I'm ready now.
Here I stand.

Formerly

The former me
cordially
invites you to move accordingly.
Keep watching and adoring,
shame on you for doubting me.
I can assure you that issuing
your versions of hexes and curses
soaked in soggy negativity
just won't do.
Retorts to my demise
is the work of fools.

Anti social social-ing,
emotional rollercoaster-ing
even with ego boasting,
it's never enough.

Be clear
that whatever you try with ill intent to do
will make all your nightmares come true
if you want to play with Santeria and Voodoo.
As the follower you are,
please excuse the former me
for allowing your comfortability.
Remain lost on the pasture among the sheep.
The chosen ones get to run
with the shadows in the trees.

Answers

What happens when I sit still?
What happens when I move?
What happens when I'm anointed
and have nothing else to prove?

What happens when it all works out
just how it's supposed to?
What happens when The Most High
whispers & says "I Told You"?

What happens when the cynics
get me rent free in their mind?
What happens when I make the best use of God's time?

What happens when my future generations speak of me?
What happens when I stop existing and start living?

What happens when I get more than what I prayed for?
What happens when I stop running and rest more?

What happens when I bury the past because I passed it?
What happens when my soul is everlasting?

What happens when my mind escapes the matrix?
What happens when my love
reaches dawns of new ages?

What happens when I'm writing my memoirs?
What happens when the universe
calls me back to the stars?

What happens when my darkness
and my light move as a collective?
What happens my angels and monsters work together?

What happens when they all see my vision?
What happens when it's all written?

What happens when I create as I speak?
What happens when I get the answers I seek?

Encrypted

My heartbeat is encrypted morse code.
Under special conditions,
is it allowed to be heard.
Each beat is a dot sequentially articulating letters
of a forever message.

My heartbeat is encrypted morse code.
One has to be attuned and in tune
with the tune of its tone
to totally innerstand the immersive experience
of what my heart is spelling- the story it's yelling.
Telling folktales & fables of reality
written too meticulous to conceive
by untrained ears and unknown hearts,
but one must conclusively correlate
its correspondence with the ether.
My magic teacher.

My heartbeat is encrypted morse code.
Using a complex combination
of beats and bumps
attuned to stops and thumps
of field frequency interference.
And when my heart resets,
blood races through my chest
telling me to sing the next chapter.

My heartbeat is encrypted morse code.
"Feel me", I say. Love's under way.
I pray one day to get the answers too.
And for everything my mind can't say,
universe hear my heart; asé.

Ayduarme

I get nervous to ask for help
because love and gratitude
is the only currency I currently have to offer
in a society that steps on love
and only values a dollar.
That's where I come up short and falter.

Usually, I don't ask for help.
Not trying to sound needy.
But it's always okay
for the people who need me
to make similar requests
instead of trying and healing.

I'm strong enough
to alchemize it though.

And I'm really not at liberty
to do it all on my own
but God guides through stoned and dirt roads.
God I trust you. My life is ours.

But for goodness sake,
give me a break.
Help is the 4 letter word
my lips have yet to make.

Party Time

I remember when "match" was a term of endearment.
Now "match" sounds like a threat because
I know it's just a battle of who can
mask their pain the best.
Who wants to drown quicker?
Who can suffer faster?
Not a match I'm ready to win.
My ancestors would be ashamed at why I'm crying.
Just imagine the amount of boulders
they had to take up off my chest;
I got the nerve to tell them I can't handle THIS?!
Now all of them adverse energies spinnin' me
and I just won't take it no more.
So I pull the white flag on that match I was in.

Mask my pain?
Not a battle I'm ready to win.
I let trees and liquor be my gate to begin.
Gate wide open to everyone else's pain,
thought I could take it so they could feel better again.
The only way I could still think I'm breathing
when swimming amongst sharks.
It was fun til' it wasn't anymore-
being the only life boat in a sea of trodden souls;
I remember when "match"
turned everyone into homies and besties-
a commonality of each crazy life.
Now "match" is a radar for me to assess
if you're a hurt one or... if you do...
really just want to have some fun.
And I get it now; after some trial,
my only error was not being me.
But I'm me now. I'm she now. I can breathe now. At peace.
"Match" still ain't no invite, but it's not a threat to me.

Airhead

I'm the mystery flavour.
You never know what's it's going to be,
but I can guarantee you'll love it.

Natural and Easy

It's easy for me to love.
I'm preconditioned to see the god in you first
unless you give me something else to believe.
No, I'm not naïve to what I can clearly perceive,
I'd simply rather love ya than feel nothing for you-
but I can surely do that too if I have to.
It's up to you, so tell God what you want to do
and I'll unequivocally oblige.

Don't be so used to pain
that pleasure feels strange when you get it.
Don't get too accustomed to disgrace and deception
leaving you with a perplexed face of rejection,
that you let your soulmate get away.

Adults tell children
"love gets complicated over time"
Complications only incur after
the mind gets compiled with excessive
compilations of "red flags, lies,
and deceptive compulsions"
causing cautions wired on the heart.

Love comes natural to me.
I naturally choose to show you the natural me.
Purely and willingly.
Look closely from a bird's eye view.

Love makes promises to us; it's our duty to keep them,
respect and receive them-
nourish and treat them with the love that Love provides.

And because it's so easy for me to love,
let my next description of it be you.

Mind

And I
I lose my mind sometimes
And when I find it
I don't mind it

Seek me
My mind's just been hiding
But when I'm writing
It gets excited

Found
Because I was crying
Subconscious lying
My mind came back again

It knows
Not to leave me
Because without my baby
I might get crazy

Stay
It understands me
Through my insanity
Tells me who I am

The best
And it only gets better
Always clever
Thank you for being near

Million Dollar Inquiry

Is chivalry alive
or has it been laid down by the riverside?

I'm in love with nostalgic times,
so I'll say it like this:
absolutely be chivalrous.

Court me.
Send me hand written love notes
through mail misted in your cologne.
Let me hold your scribes in my palms
feeling the warmth of happy tears
cascading down my cheeks,
preparing my stationery
to write you back.

Make me music
and turn me into timeless art.
Hypnotize me with songs' cadence.
Get creative.
Walk with me along sea shore
only paused by sweet kisses
as the moon gives us her blessing.

Bring me flowers and plants.
Bouquets to fill my vases
and big greenery to fill any corners
in my home that have empty spaces.

Support my passions, missions, and visions
with solutions and assistance
the same way I'll do yours.

From minute to grand gestures,
I appreciate them all
with supreme gratitude and pleasure-
as an exemplary lady should.

Be extravagantly courteous and kind;
I don't mind. I wouldn't have it any other way.
Surprise me with experiences
I've never had before.

And of course....
keep me on the proper side of the sidewalk
and always open my door.

Enola

They wonder why I'm usually alone.

Because I don't have hide from me.
No need to pretend.
My aloneness is where I can be myself;
whoever I am,
extraordinary abnormalities.
The universe and I talk;
we share walks around galaxies.

I'm not in battle with the facade of societal existence
to who I must project.
My soul knew, tried and true,
what it was getting into-
entering a body in this time and space.
It used to pull at my spirit.
25 revolving cycles, I didn't want to hear it.

They wonder why I'm usually alone.

Because my love is only felt when it's gone.
I'm that orisha, that deity.
I must be an enigma;
one forever unknown.

An "idea" of me is loved
but they're too scared to hold.
I'm like Excalibur, placed by the ancients
to be marveled by commoners.

Red alert, all eyes avert!
Too many people "peopleing",
not enough souls living soulfully.
The current world isn't ready for me
... at least not in this dystopian blip.

I'll be the angel for my descendants
and leave remnants of repentance.
So few things deserve apologies.

They wonder why I'm usually alone.

Because I never cower from a trial or challenge,
but I have bigger battles to conquer than
focusing on seeing hollowed bodies eye to eye.

How High

God said:
"Trust Me"

I replied not with words,
but with the spring of my feet
farther from the ground than I've ever been.

God touched my head and replied:
"You're ready my child"

Way to Express

I'd rather put it in this poem.
Pieces of everything me.
Not closed. Not hiding.
A full honesty policy.

Caught in between
these human genes
of wanting to explain to you, me
and feeling like I shouldn't have to
because you should be studying.
Goddess 101.

Heart chakra open.
Bridge flowing. Boat rowing.
Floating on a sea of words;
space between every letter
is where I come up for breath
and energy to say the rest.
Voice becomes softer
as I control my breathing.
An anomaly of properly conjugated verbs,
synonymously a palate of refreshing herbs
to cleanse body with soul and connect to spirit.
Everything a woman should be.
So esoteric that I'm not a person,
I'm a frequency.
You must tune in to speak to me.

A cala lily which bloomed from concrete
where bullets meant to penetrate,
ricochet off me and still I rise.

Not out the mud.
But rooted deeply in quicksand
growing tall and strong
while being pulled down by man.

No lifeboat, no raft, or helping hand.
Only me, God, and love figuring out a plan.

In lieu of overexposing,
I prefer to put it all in this poem
and let the way Mahogany Speaks
be the typewriter of my soul.

Stupid Questions

"Are you alright?"
What does that even mean?
I'm all left, all up, all down.
Now tell me what you really want to ask.
Because what are you gonna do if I say I'm not?
Are you gonna bend my L's into straight lines?
Bring me back to earth when I float away?
Pick me up when I'm down?
You asked, signaled from my expressions,
indicative that something clearly is not all-right.
With narrow sight and all my might...

"How are you? How you doing? How are things?"
Break this down.
Is it that you really have something to say?
Are you actually concerned about my response?
Or is your brain drowned
in societal syrup of robotic tendencies?
Because if you had a real question for me,
you just may get a real response.
The context of these inquiries is a programming error
that would make AI look like the real intelligence.

Now do yourself a favour,
don't ask me those ridiculous questions again.
Your reminder
that my response
will be something you couldn't even decipher.

On a Haiku Pt. 1

I broke free from the crowds.
Now I can only be around sparingly.
Maybe even not at all.

An old self-toxic trait of mine:
Forcing myself to suffer deeper in
Punishment from choices I knew better than to make.

222

Double up my 2's and get my 4's for protection.
Intense trial and error,
now no more second guessing.

Right time right place.
Had to sit still here.
I emptied self to build me up;
change internally
before I could switch the scenery.
Had to love myself more than I ever did before
to stop getting in my own way
and open up the doors
even when I wasn't sure.

Shot fear in the face with 2 22's.
No place for disrespect to my love temple
not from anyone or especially from my mental.
Would I be farther along if in the past I listened?
I'm not stuck, I'm in optimal position
just like the moon when she shines
and makes the night glisten.

Here and now is where:
I embraced the goddess,
started to really model,
opened my first businesses,
and became a better word artist.
Just to name a few.

At times, I think about my king and who he will be.
I send my love through the moon for the time being.
Always, I pray for strength to protect my family.
I ponder what to name my next chapter
& where it'll take me.

From 396 to 963 Hz,
the frequencies and singing bowls
help me do the work.
Celebrate the moon.

Align my field with the solstices, eclipses,
and equinoxes too.
Let Zen Buddhism and Taoism be The Way.
Thich Nhat Hanh, Shi Heng Yi,
Confucius, and Lao Tzu.

One with the elements and seasons,
let nature do its work.
Spirit animal always by my side.
More than dropping jewels,
I'm laying out rare pearls.

Here's some insight into my life,
how Anahata came to be;
I'm the bridge between lower and higher energies.
Take notes and you might learn a thing or... 2.

If you ever met me before,
you didn't know me then.
Now certainly you can't comprehend.
To be in my presence or have my love
is an honour. A deep privilege
Quite unfortunate for you to mistakenly waste it.

My love is still infinite,
my Love Temple is selective.
Only true peacekeepers know the password.
6 clicks, 3 pairs, right in the perfect place on time
I'm 2(too)2 protected.
2:22

Shower Therapy

I didn't know I could drown standing tall
until I felt my lungs filling up.
A heavy piece of energy shedding from me
and suffocating my sadness
to take it all and run.
Grabbing my chest,
tears running down my face
as shower water mixes in its place;
I may have well been in space
while the oxygen from my body escaped.

I wept from the pain I made her endure.
Infuriated by the agony she let me tolerate.
She welded a giant rusty anchor
to my sternum and proceeded to add pressure
by strength training my lungs
from straining my breaths.
Preposterous conquests.

I wished she could be more than what she was.
More than a passenger in her life.
More than an extra to her own movie.
More than being told she can't drive
and without negating, she accepts.
More than a:
"break the glass in case of emergency"
More than a child trapped in experience,
allowing those who can't even lead
to dictate who'd she turn out to be.

And simply be the light
that gleamed from her eyes at birth.
She forgot she was the star.

Daughter of the water who couldn't swim.
And I counted on it.
I was ready for her to drown.
Alleviate me.
I couldn't fight, flee, or scream.
We both knew what was happening.

She had to go.
I was molting.

Almost seemed like an impossible feat
and possibly the purest feeling I've ever known.
"I forgive you", I told her;
observing her grey shadow
disappear down the drain.

Haiku Hour Pt. 2

Here's a secret about poets:
If we've never written anything about you,
We probably didn't like you that much.

You could take it for face value,
You could find the deeper meaning,
Or you could do both.

Zeros and Ones

101 reasons, 101 lessons
101 seasons, 101 guesses.
Revolutions of trial to try all that comes forth.
Head aches from pain and too much Tylenol
Where's the detour?
Not the scenic route
because I've seen it all before.
Just need some answers. Bring them right now.
Patience hasn't paid me not a dollop of dollars
or a sprinkle of cents.
So answer me this: is this recipe faulty?
But don't fault me.
They do say that's just the way things go.

And who is "they"?
"They" don't know.
Faces "they" won't show.
"They" built a dome for me to be trapped in
where love can't grow.

Damn, maybe that's why my head hurts.
Going around in circles
because my oxygen is cut off.
I've waited long enough,
but "they" may say no if I ask.
So what will happen if I just go and
break the glass?

Rain On Me

I don't always know what to do
or which choice is best to make.
Yet what I do have, is love. I have faith.
Your power and grace.

I apologize,
with every atom of stardust I'm made of,
for every time I've ever questioned your methods.

Deepest gratitude for your forgiveness
when I miss my mark.
I serve no god, but the one inside me-
the one almighty.
You're guiding
and that's why I'm thriving.
The one source of course.
If what I want isn't what I need,
save me from my transgressions.

Say jump.
I won't question
because I trust that I will fly
God, you've been showing off-
bringing all these blessings in.
Allow me to repay by showing favour
to all that which you've created.

Sensitive

Sensitive-
Origin: Latin.
Derivative: French.
Definition: Capable of sensation. The ability to feel.

Are you saying you cannot?

SEN-SIT-IVE
9 letters like the root in feminine- femiNINE.
The essence of a goddess should be such.
Truly defined.
This life chose me.
I'm supposed be
the energy
you speak life into-
the one you're akin to
thinly veiled for big views.

Yes I'm sensitive, so what?

To the words and to the touch.
It's usually better
when I'm to myself for protection.
You've just been made hard
from the pain of passive aggression.
Intuition broken, so you don't know who to let in.

I'm the only one to make you realize
how reckless at the to tongue you've been
and make you take 10-
rethink how you speak to me.

Yes I'm sensitive, and your point?

I see clearer, feel more, and think deeper.
I act calmer, listen more, a loving creature.
... what The Universe intended.

Would you trample a garden
to make the flowers grow?
Or maybe it helps that I cry more
so the petals feel happy to show.

I'm "sensitive"... I get it ...

And you got damn right!
Never to imagine a life where
I COULDN'T feel vibrations
coursing through my blood
and making my heart dance.
Or slowly dying from acidic tears
burning my insides that I'm forced to keep in.
That would be a sad existence.
I feel what you could never and see what you don't.

So yes, I'm sensitive.

Guilty is charged.
Felony in the first degree
for feeling so much
so passionately.
I take this sentence to the chin
in the name of sensitivity.
You could lock my body up
in the prison of society
but my soul floats free.

You know, the "sensitive" me.

Now They All Love Water

Being a water sign
means I'm multilingual,
but most people seem to have
forgotten how water works.

I do my water work
with my water works.
And make water shirts
yet hard water hurts.
Speak bad on water
and make watered dirt.
But good energy will show you
what this water's worth.

A water sign, a "cancer", it's in my DNA.
scoff now or forever hold your peace.

But remember next time
you think about water adversely,
the same water you drink to save your life
could also drown you in the sea.

Home

Sometimes home doesn't even feel safe anymore.
Like I can't breathe free and just be me
when the circulation of energy is off alignment.
Readjusting, realigning, repositioning,
reworking, restarting, rewinding...
So much "re" that I sound like a scratched record.
But with each scratch, a bit of progress seems to fall off.
Home should see me for who I am.
Home is supposed to feel free-
like my sanctuary, where I can be me without question.
But all I do is get questions and be questioned
on why my existence
doesn't fit the current pattern of home anymore.
Like home is actually on a quest
to hear my responses to those questions,
but instead I get shunned for what I say.
Home doesn't speak my language
and won't learn so I can feel heard,
but I grow deeper and faster than home can catch up
so I have to learn just to accept that.
Home tends to ask "what's wrong"
as if finding a different frequency is always bad.
I always have to adjust to home
instead of home adjusting to me.

War

The longest war I ever fought
was Armageddon to say the least.
Mental, emotional, physical.
Scars, wounds, tears, and scabs-
never caused by a man,

but the relationship with self.
My echo, my shadow, and me.
My shadow and me echoing
heinous atrocities at each other.
The deeper the sadness,
the more bitter tears taste.

I had a rabid habit
of rapidly accessing tragedy.
Haphazardly relying on travesty
for excuses to be mad at me.
How noble in reason
could a piece of work that's man be?
No form of nobility in accepting defeat.
That's all I expected of me.
Rejecting movement, acquiescing to excuses.
How foolish I was, but never will be.

CHAPTER 3:

SCALE OUT

Love's Leftovers

How do you know love past all the smoke and mirrors
of sweet words and even sweeter kisses?
What's love after the flesh has had a taste of passion
and the tongue is finished pursuing
explorations of tantalizing explosions
from discovering the crevices of secrets?
Is this even what you feel?
Does the sex heal?
Is the love real?

Is it really love if the depths of how you connect
land on shallow surfaces?
Plateauing on rewinded vcr tapes of regurgitated emotions.
And still, you say it's love.
But what's love to you past saying: "I love, I do, I choose"?

What's left of love after the feast?
Preparing to eat well, picking at the leftovers,
& trashing the spoils until the fridge is empty.
You give thanks for taking and not replenishing.
Gluttony in its highest degree- overconsumption of energy.

Can you really know love
if you can't build more together than feelings?
Revolving your life around them casually
without creating something to hold tangibly...
to create is to love.
If utilized properly,
love builds a metaphysical monopoly of true source.
But without foundation,
you both are left separately pulling from chaos.
Entropy will find more entropy.

So if the love stops, was it ever really love?

Emitting Time

Time is a fabricated fallacy
that we all get tricked tragically
into pledging our allegiance.
The perfect anagram.

Emit Time

A linear regression.
Items of time emit mites of pressure
to make the soul feel lesser
never greater or better
until a little becomes a lot
and the storm is too much.
Already prayed to the lord soul to take.
Drop unnecessary dead weight.

Privileged

I love with expensive taste.
To love me requires an exquisite palate.
I don't dabble in mediocre love.

Disconnect

What's found in disconnect
is a life lived separate since it's widely believed
that what's done to soul has no effect on the body
in a sense and vice versa.

Phase 1, peel your skeleton out from the inside.
Now it hangs on the wall that becomes decoration
for skeptics praying for a whirlwind of your downfalls.

Phase 2, your soul leaves-
exhausted from exhausting and exerting
the best from all of your worst things.
With no bones, the flesh becomes too heavy
for your soul to breathe and there's no other way out
than to watch you from afar suffering.

Phase 3 is fatality.
A body without a brace that lacks life-
skin draping the floor lost to living.
Death by a thousand cuts and a thousand steps,
exposed flesh unprepared and unprotected to the rest.
So now it's "Just existing. Just trending. Just sex.
Just whatever comes next".

They throw stones at your bones.
Spirit cries at the pain a flesh can no longer feel
since your nerves turned into play things on the wall
next to your skeleton wheel.

Who Are You?

If you can tell me who you are
without telling me what you do,
that's someone I can respect
because you know you.

Misdirection

He's angry with love.
Probably because he still hasn't ascended into a man
worth having a woman
who's not pretending when she's with him.
He's only a nigga:
Never
Intending
God's
Gracious
Altitudes
and he claims to be the realest at it.
Really the realest addict
divided and subtracted from sense (cents),
he could never add it. Love ain't in his equation.

She's upset with love.
Not because "he" did it.
It's that she hasn't earned her womanhood-
befitting a lady who he calls his goddess.
She's just a bitch:
Beast
Inside
The
Creator's
House
And she's bad with it, so she says.
Bad at it and getting worse these days.
Conjoined hex and curse-
tried to form a compound compliment but the problem is,
she internalized a weaponized projection.

How can one be stagnant, yet so demanding of love?
Looks as if her and him both caught up in
misdirection.

Unknown Surprises

The unknown excites my spirit.
Surprises intrigue my soul.
Change makes me feel alive.
Risk prevents me from growing old.

The Final Hour

A lot of love happens at dusk
and I must
be obliged to take credit.

My slow burnout really says it-
they know it's my time to go.
Where will inspiration go?
May they show their resilience.

Last times are just next times-
"until the next time we meet
in another dimension",
I say shifting my radiance
from dandelion
to a sorbet of soft embers.
I've made up my mind, this is my sky.
This may be my last set
but it's only my first rise.

Home Base

So many mega money hands
sending love over seas,
but what about the families right here?

Have you helped home base be better?
Gave our youth a meal and a sweater
or would you prefer the facade
of merely looking kind and clever?

I absolutely praise the very day
our entire planet's safe
but IN THIS MOMENT,
efforts are more impactful
to our people on home base.

You see across the sea what's happening
from a series of TV's and phone screens –
brain binding only to what's blatantly
broadcasting into your pupils.

Numb to all atrocities in your backyard;
be the person you needed growing up
    for another soul who feels like it's too tough.

Bellies starve, hearts hurt,
and bodies drop every single day...
our war is just covered in propaganda.

You turn a blind eye
and only cry at what's televised...
Can you remember
what Mos Def said his Umi Says?
"Want my people to be free, that's all that matters to me"

Right here on home base,
there's an unquenchable thirst for greed-
an unsatisfiable need for gluttony
that infects the mind with dopamine shots
from throwing scraps at causes
that don't take any real power to help impact.

If you care so deeply about international turmoil,
talk to people like Chaka Bars
and take your million dollar donations
directly to their soil.

Or how about we fix, as a collective,
what's in the midst of home base?
Support the X For Boys school
that teaches young melanated men aren't anyone's toy
and every part of them is valuable, not something to destroy.

Spend a day in the hoods with New Era Nation
helping families feel protected and safe;
build lasting programs in every city and state.
Buy blocks of bandos and blighted businesses
to show our men, women, and children
what building together really is...

AND THEN

we can go overseas together
to make it really shake.
Show our distant brothers and sisters
that their well being is no one's to take.
Every saddened country empathized for
can be helped made safe.
But only after we fix home base.

Too Tight

Holding on to love
that doesn't want to be kept
is like:
forcing quiet breaths as adrenaline pumps
or a ponytail unbearably tight.
Swimming outside in the winter
or napping in a hot car, windows rolled up.
Attempting to lose weight on a salad
9 parts toppings and 1 part lettuce
or paying extra taxes to the IRS.
Biting your tongue twice on the same side
or punching the wall you hit your toe on...

What part is supposed to make sense?
Lover or captor, you choose.

Inspired Alchemy

When Aretha Franklin sang "Ain't No Way",
I felt it in my soul just like that.
But she hit notes I wouldn't dare,
so I have to say it with my heart.

La niña de oro con ojos oros nosotros
somos loco con pasión.
Silver heart, copper eyes
mesmerized by current times.
Currents, tides
concurrent lines
congruent sides
See all that for what is mine.
I sing with silent songs.

Haunted House

Is it still called life
if the entire being
is stripped from its core
and exists just enough
to not turn into dust?

Can one be alive if
all parts that make soul and body,
separate- absent among land?

Spec by spec,
the soul evacuates,
exhausted from exhausting and exerting
all of the worst things.

It has no home
in the body anymore,
so it wanders away
to ease the suffering.
Another lost soul.

A hollow shell of flesh remains shackled
to the bones without a life sentence
because there's no life left.

All the least charming
aspects of existing
creep inside
like a night cap at an air bnb.

Secret clubhouse
not a secret anymore.
Just a party spot for pain
and a nest for the virus of regret
to live again.

A tear from those
forced to watch a wonderful vessel be wasted.
And a tear to those
whose only desire is to take from it.
Another suffered body.

The flesh has been stretched,
flipped, and flattened.
Left melted in cracks on the floor
making tracks straight to the museum of bones
where a life once lived.

A saddened gaze at the skeletons
remaining engraved to the walls
-separated from it all.
Decoration for the watchers.

"Here hangs a display
of exactly
what abusing life gets"
....

J.F.H.

Let's go to a place where the past doesn't exist.

It's dangerous back there and safer in the unknown.

Let's live in a moment compiled of other moments

making miraculous marks across the Milky Way.

In this new place, all that matters is love.

Blessed to live in joy, fun, and happiness eternally

– our birthright.

The spirit guides wait for us there.

Midsummer

I may be a little crazy.
I drink hot tea in 98°
down south summer heat.

Dragonflies Talk

Dragonflies have large eyes
that let them see almost 360°.

Muscles attached directly to their wings
allowing them faster flight over any insect,
truly amazing beings.

They move in ways no other can:
forward and cross, backward and hover
all in place with such grace.

But here's the secret you may have missed:
dragonflies use their flight pattern
to spell messages in cursive.

I found out on a glorious day in May
when my spirit animal came to visit me.

Slow down the fast flies of little dragon
with your eyes to read messages
you've been sent from the angels.

Tomorrow

The one day we never get is tomorrow.
Tomorrow never comes.
Saying over and over:
"I'll get to it tomorrow. Tomorrow for sure."
Putting myself in a state of despondent conflict,
in limbo of yesterday and now.
Hurting myself for not already having it done,
yet still not doing.
What is tomorrow?
As we exist in this dimension
that is rightfully the present.
When do we go to tomorrow?
And if we never actually get to the place
when we say we'll make it happen,
live our dreams,
and love freely,
where do we go until then?

Altitude

How many people have seen you, bird?
Wished to be you
Breathe your air
And put their hopes on your wings

How many eyes have watched you, bird?
Longing to behold your view
And feel your freedom

How many songs have been sung to you, bird?
Echoed hymns
Seeking interpretation

How many believe you to be their angel, bird?
Telephone to god
Who keeps their prayers secret

If I am never to see you again, bird
Sink your talons into my immortal being
Spread pieces of me onto the earth

You Only Live Forever

I want to take a risk...
do something I've never done before.
It's time to take a chance.
I need to explore.
A change of change.
Familiar thoughts estranged
from a longing for what's new.

Optimize & Upgrade

How do you optimize your happiness?
By still finding ways to smile
through set backs and outages;
these are times to get creative.
Show the universe what you can do
given the hand you have.
Circumstance is but a matter of man.

Post-Nuptial Disagreements

It's unwise for a wife to put her husband in position
of forcing executive order of what's best for him
versus the feelings of his wife at the cost of his happiness.
And anybody who would create feelings like that
in the seedling of a relationship
will do it well into a long partnership harvest crop.

Quite apparently marriage isn't for most.
It's only, solely [soully], and wholly [holy]
for those whose intuition can dimensionally
decipher the angel from the leech.
Choosing to document a partnership is meant to seal
in scribe a testament of who both have already promised to be.
Love with infinite flavourings. Safe space to breathe.

How can she be at ease when his nervous system
spikes cortisol into everything he thinks around her
so he's never at peace?
As their numbers of suns and moons grow together,
tranquility in their union is supposed to increase.

How can she claim love for him if her heart beats otherwise?
Marriage should be real, not rumored in disguise.
His emotional treasure chest deserves unwavering respect,
with or without his physical assets
as long as his soul comes correct.

This is to be discovered before marriage.
Dare each other to learn who lives inside.
Does the puzzle piece fit or is it forced to comply?

A husband who's earned his wife's peace prize
shouldn't have to feel unsettled when he looks into her eyes.

Still Too Loud

Universe, forgive my mind
for every time
I keep asking for answers.
Praying for clarity
and quiet thoughts
amidst subconscious banter.

Have mercy on my heart
each moment
I miss the signs, messages, and omens
as my brain makes it impossible
for my soul to hear.
An irrational irrelevant cacophony
of noise bombarding me
which I practice diligently
to keep at bay.

State of Emergency

Everything is ALL FINE everyone!
Nothing to see here.
It's all okay.
Fan out and keep separating
back to your regularly scheduled programming.
Our people are doing GREAT!
Don't you see it?

You know...
how we're still having the same conversations
on participating in everything degrading,
yet won't do better and still end up hating.
Most of our people still treating a dollar
better than a sister, mother, brother, or father.

Now you KNOW...
how we can all share similar stories
of what our hoods were like
and what "every black household had"
while every hood to this very day looks exactly the same
and nothing has changed.

Don't tell me you DON'T know...
How just 50-60 years ago, we had vigor to take charge.
Our leaders were ferocious;
those who followed were relentless.

Assata Shakur gave years
of her physical freedom willingly to liberation.
Thought her people would continue to fight
for the sacrifices she made and lead in her place.
Now black pride only leaks through
corners in these spaces.

Gil Scott Heron prophesied
the revolution would not be televised.
It's artificially automated, mobilized, digitized.
Simulation and simulacra. Where's the real?

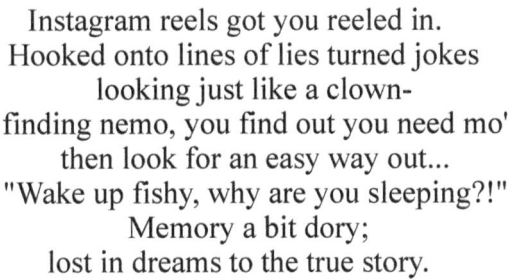

Instagram reels got you reeled in.
Hooked onto lines of lies turned jokes
looking just like a clown-
finding nemo, you find out you need mo'
then look for an easy way out...
"Wake up fishy, why are you sleeping?!"
Memory a bit dory;
lost in dreams to the true story.

Sister Souljah's voice pierced power
in painful places
of pale people with soggy souls and indifferent faces.
She knew how bad we needed to escape
from massa's rat races.
Can we finally make those changes?
Decorated like our predecessors-
same scars on our skin.
War wounds bleeding out, no love pouring in.
Reminders of where we left off
& where we need to begin.
A new reckoning.

What's left to respect? Who's left to protect?
The children are our saviours.
How do we show them proper love
if we're replicating destructive behaviours?
Let's make our youth baby panthers
instead of baby daddies and baby mommas.
Unhealed adults raising kids
is a recipe for generations of more trauma.

Enough BEEN enough.
Are you down to uplift your people?
Stand by their side,
watch their back from the frontline,
and never leave them behind?

I'm ready for a new conversation.
The one where we build
utopia for our descendants.
Rule the land that was always ours
and teach "we are family"
is more than just a sentence.

Smoke

Sit silently at sunrise
stare at the stretch of incense smoke
watch it send coded notes
No two patterns ever mimic
like little flakes of snow

Because I Can See...

Now that my eyes are open,

I can give attention to the beauty of the world.
Life speaks clearly
and its vibrations coat my ears and silk.

Because I can see now,

the sun is no longer a flicker of light
strolling shadows of the past across my perception.
I've left the cave.

I can't remember colour looking like this –
a gorgeous glow gleaming gracefully.

Now that I can see,

the only time I'll ever need to close my eyes
is so to dream and lock in the memories
of contrasting magnificence.

On a Haiku Pt. 2

Even when it feels unseen,
It's seen
With much certainty.

Not all the time, is there something to say.
It's okay to simply let quiet take place
And fast from unnecessary words.

About Nature

You see, the thing about nature...

is that she's really your best confidante.
Comrade Compadre Co-mingling Coexisting
Wherever you are, she's there.

She never complains when you don't listen
as she sings stellar songs,
yet, will always be your ear.
She loves you regardless.
Her trees aren't thanked for their service
yet, are ever present.
Her grass never cries as it's cut and trampled
yet, grows in grace
and absorbs your sadness when you need grounding.

Nature takes the omniscient seat.
Holds no grudges for the pain thrust upon her.

And unlike people,
the thing about nature is that there aren't hesitations
or inquisitions on the quality of love or compassion in her hugs.
She knows the real you.

Nature is never long distance.
And even if you ignore her presence
right until the moment you need her essence,
nature is still omnipotent and omnipresent.

She's forever in your corner,
in your back yard, up the block at the park,
flying, floating, flowing, and free.

Toxic Positivity

It becomes easier to be positive for others
and put on a front as if you're renewed
when it's far from even fair condition.
But it's better to fake the fun.
Your happiness is really a hoax.

Everything inside
is falling apart and crumbling.
They're deaf to cries
& blind to sad eyes.
Unable to love what they can't see or feel.

You struggle to put your own pieces together;
each looks the same.
The mask is suffocating.
Even smiling starts to feel toxic.

Understand/Overstand

If you truly feel like everything you do
and/or
everyone you encounter that didn't last in your life
"wasted your time",
then you living this life itself must also be time wasted.

Everything happens for a reason,

… We are all still souls taking baby steps
and everything learn is to be blessed.

Psychiatric Assistance

We're all delusional.
Merely writing about love feels better
in a sense because we get to experience
all of our fantasies
in escaping this illusionary reality.

A Trillion Choices

I could talk about
the systematic oppression of my people.
And how we were clearly gods
who let all our prizes on earth be taken
by mental castration.

Or how most people are sheep
barked at by sheep dogs
controlled by shepards
owned by puppeteers
made by the hidden ones-
so many levels to hypnotized manipulation.

I could even talk about the pain of my past,
trauma I chose, consequences of my reactions,
and sequences of suffering,
but we all have a "story" to carry
and those trying to "be special" are far too ordinary...

So I'd rather talk about Love-
its implicating temptations and insinuations of attempted abuse.
How Love gets degraded and manipulated
into a revolving door of oversaturated hatred.
Love doesn't deserve to be misused.

Those bad choices people infuse and confuse
with Love make the idea of sleeping on thorns
be better to choose.
And that couldn't be further from the truth.
Traps of tricks and trials
trying to hide the tears of their inner child crying.

And Love didn't create that shame.
Love didn't make that pain.

Love pulls reigns
to save the stallion from cliff jumping
but only when it's tame, can it listen.

So hard it's fighting and trying,
yet Love is on life support-
suffering in silence at masses of constant violence.
But I refuse to resort
to discord and discourse put on Love;
don't annihilate the best part of being alive.

I would prefer to speak on Love.
How beautiful Love is and its energy in motion.
It's elegant yet wild and eclectic,
like Love at first sight and a connection that's magnetic.
... but only if it's protected.

So while they carry a cadence to Love
of hate, hurt, and apathy,
I'd rather be Love's hummingbird harmony.
Modified & calibrated,
reverberating a language that echoes through infinity-
fabulous figure 8 shaping.
And honestly, I've tried to be the grinch.
But to say plainly, it's draining.
Carrying loads of disdain
for a past slowly erasing is a mistake I'm not making.

I choose Love.
Marvelous to feel.
Love cures what time can't heal.
Yes, still
I choose to talk about Love.

ABOUT THE AUTHOUR

The Goddess Anahata (given name: Mahogany M. Shelton) opened her publishing company, LUNAR LEVELS PUBLISHING, in June 2023.

LLP is available to all new & emerging authours/artists who make works of poetry, prose, romance, and all various creative literature. LLP also offers free publishing education to indie authours and has a free e-book for new writers in the form of a step by step 6 week guide to becoming self published.

Love's Promise is The Goddess' second poetry collection from LUNAR LEVELS PUBLISHING, followed by her first collection entitled *Lunar Eclipse: The Anthology of Emerging Emotions & Revolutions of Love* which is available on every major online retailer (including Barnes & Noble, Books-A-Million, Amazon, Google Books, Ingram Spark, bookshop.org) and worldwide. *Lunar Eclipse* has reached the UK, Sweden, Canada, India, Nigeria, and Germany with plans to expand global distribution for both current and all future books.

The Goddess Anahata can be seen performing these pieces live all across the country with large fan bases of Peacekeepers in Michigan, Kentucky, California, New York, Pennsylvania, and Illinois. More than a poet, The Goddess Anahata has taken her melodically hypnotizing voice to music- making her poems into songs. Her newest EP "Lunar Eclipse Vol. 1" and two vibrant singles are available on all streaming platforms (including Spotify, Apple Music, iTunes, Tidal, Amazon Music, Even.Biz, Deezer, Bandcamp, Audiomack, & YouTube Music).

"Poetry is the gift we receive to transform the limitation of words into a digestible emotions for human and cosmic expansion. What we create is not only for ourselves and we must be conscious of the emotions we invoke in others", says The Goddess. Studying from the greats and building a legacy that lasts for generations, she knows there is much more work to be done and infinitely more art to create.

The world is one; everything is a poem.

www.ingramcontent.com/pod-product-compliance
Lightning Source LLC
Chambersburg PA
CBHW020307010526
44107CB00001B/12